Dear PJ Library Families,

You might wonder why PJ Library® has chosen *A Tree Is Nice* as one of its selections. What, you may ask, is inherently Jewish about this book? After all, no Jewish holiday or activity is observed in its pages, and there is no Hebrew language or mention of Israel. *A Tree Is Nice* is included in PJ Library because the premise, content and messages of the book – appreciation for the innate beauty of a tree, the expression of nature's bounty in a tree's fruits, the use of trees for the shelter and protection of God's creatures, human and otherwise – are basic to Jewish thought and action. The gentle ideas expressed in the book should and do transcend any religion or life practice, yet they are intrinsically Jewish. Environmental awareness through conservation, reuse, and recycling has been and continues to be a Jewish imperative; now more than ever, this mindfulness is critical and must be transmitted from one generation to the next. We hope this book inspires your family to consider and act in concert with nature in new and meaningful ways.

A TREE
IS NICE

by

JANICE MAY UDRY

pictures by

MARC SIMONT

■ HarperCollins*Publishers*

Text copyright © 1956 by Janice Udry
Text copyright renewed 1984 by Janice May Udry
Pictures copyright © 1956 by Marc Simont
Pictures copyright renewed 1984 by Marc Simont
Manufactured in China. All rights reserved.
For information address HarperCollins Children's Books, a division
of HarperCollins Publishers, 10 East 53rd Street, New York, NY 10022.
Library of Congress Catalog Card Number: 56-5153
ISBN 978-0-06-196280-6 (pbk.)
12 13 14 15 SCP 10 09 08 07 06 05 04 03 02

Trees are very nice. They fill up the sky.

They go beside the rivers and down the valleys. They live up on the hills.

Trees make the woods.
They make everything beautiful.

Even if you have just one tree, it is nice too.
A tree is nice because it has leaves. The leaves
whisper in the breeze all summer long.

In the fall, the leaves come down and we play in them. We walk in the leaves and roll in the leaves.

We build playhouses out of the leaves. Then we pile them up with our rakes and have a bonfire.

A tree is nice because it has a trunk and limbs.
We can climb the tree and see over all the yards.
We can sit on a limb and think about things.
Or play pirate ship up in the tree.

If it is an apple tree we can climb it
to pick the apples.

Cats get away from dogs by going up the tree.
Birds build nests in trees and live there.
Sticks come off the trees too.
We draw in the sand with the sticks.

A tree is nice to hang a swing in.

Or a basket of flowers.

It is a good place to lean your hoe while you rest.

A tree is nice because it makes shade.

The cows lie down in the shade when it is hot.

People have picnics there too. And the baby
takes his nap in his buggy in the shade.

A tree is nice for a house to be near.
The tree shades the house and keeps it cool.

The tree holds off the wind and keeps the wind
from blowing the roof off the house sometimes.

A tree is nice to plant. You dig the biggest
hole you can and put the little tree in.
Then you pour in lots of water and then the dirt.
You hang the shovel back in the garage.

Every day for years and YEARS
you watch the little tree grow.
You say to people, "I planted that tree."

They wish they had one so they
go home and plant a tree too.